BEST OF THE ROLLING STONES

VOLUME ONE 1963-1973

D1427460

ANGIE
PAGE SEVEN

AS TEARS GO BY
PAGE TEN

BROWN SUGAR
PAGE THIRTEEN

GET OFF MY CLOUD
PAGE SIXTEEN

GOOD TIMES, BAD TIMES
PAGE EIGHTEEN

HONKY TONK WOMEN
PAGE TWENTY

JUMPIN' JACK FLASH
PAGE TWENTY-TWO

LADY JANE
PAGE TWENTY-FOUR

LET'S SPEND THE NIGHT TOGETHER
PAGE TWENTY-SIX

MIDNIGHT RAMBLER
PAGE THIRTY

PAINT IT BLACK
PAGE THIRTY-EIGHT

RUBY TUESDAY
PAGE FORTY

SATISFACTION
PAGE FORTY-TWO

SHE'S A RAINBOW
PAGE FORTY-FIVE

STREET FIGHTING MAN
PAGE FORTY-EIGHT

SYMPATHY FOR THE DEVIL
PAGE FIFTY-TWO

STAR STAR
PAGE FIFTY-EIGHT

19TH NERVOUS BREAKDOWN
PAGE SIXTY-ONE

TUMBLING DICE
PAGE SIXTY-FOUR

UNDER MY THUMB
PAGE SIXTY-NINE

ANGIE

WORDS & MUSIC BY MICK JAGGER & KEITH RICHARD

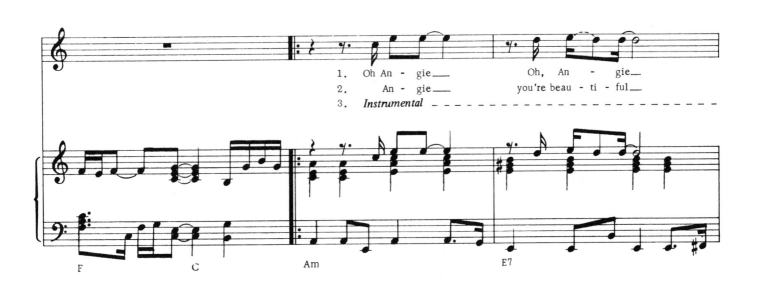

1. Oh An - gie___ Oh, An - gie___
2. An - gie___ you're beau - ti - ful___
3. *Instrumental* _ _ _ _ _ _ _ _ _

when will those dark clouds dis-ap-pear___ An - gie___ An -
but ain't it time we said good-bye___ An - gie___ I
_ _ _ _ _ _ _ _ _ _ _ _ _ _ _ 4. (D.S.) *Instrumental* _ _ _ _ _

AS TEARS GO BY

WORDS & MUSIC BY MICK JAGGER, KEITH RICHARD & ANDREW LOOG OLDHAM

It is the eve - ning of the day,
My rich - es can't buy ev - 'ry - thing,

I sit and watch the chil - dren play.
I want to hear the chil - dren sing.

Smil - ing fac - es I can see but not for me,
All I hear is the sound

BROWN SUGAR

WORDS & MUSIC BY MICK JAGGER & KEITH RICHARD

Moderate tempo (32 bars per minute)

Gold— Coast slave— ship bound for
Beat - ing,— cold Eng-lish
I bet your ma-ma was a

cot - ton fields,— sold— in a mar-ket down in New Or - leans.— Scarred
blood runs hot,— la — dy of the house won-d'rin where it's gon-na stop. House
Tent Show queen,— and — all her girl friends were sweet six - teen. — I'm

GET OFF OF MY CLOUD

WORDS & MUSIC BY MICK JAGGER & KEITH RICHARD

I live in an a-part-ment on the nine-ty ninth floor of my block
tele-phone is ring-in' I say "Hi it's me Who's there on the line?"
sick and tired, fed up with this and de-cided to take a drive down town.

And I sit at home lookin' out the win-dow im-ag-in-in' the world has
A voice says, "Hi hullo. How are you? Well I guess I'm doing
It was so very quiet and peaceful. There was no-body, not a soul a-

stopped
fine
-round

Then in flies a guy thats all dress'd
He says, "It's three a.m. and there's too much noise Don't you
I laid my-self out I was so

GOOD TIMES, BAD TIMES

WORDS & MUSIC BY MICK JAGGER & KEITH RICHARD

There've been good times, there've been bad times I've had my share of hard times too

But I lost my__ faith in the world__ Hon - ey when I__ lost you.

Re-mem-ber the good times_____ we had to - geth-er__

HONKY TONK WOMEN

WORDS AND MUSIC BY MICK JAGGER, KEITH RICHARD, BILL WYMAN,
CHARLIE WATTS AND BRIAN JONES.

(1) I met a gin soaked bar — room queen — in Mem-phis,
laid a div-or-cee — in New — York Cit - y,

She tried — to take—me up — stairs — for a ride. —
I had to put up some — kind — of a fight. —

She had to heave me right — a - cross—her should — er,
The la - dy then she cov - ered me — with ros — es,

'Cos I just ____ can't seem ____ to drink ____ you off ____ my ____ mind
She blew my nose, ____ and then ____ she blew ____ my ____ mind

C   G   D7

(Chorus)   It's the Honk _____ ky Tonk

G   G   D

Wo -men   Gim-me, gim-me, gim-me the honk-y tonk ____

G   G   D

1

blues.   (2) I   LAST   blues.

G   G   C C#dim G Am7 G

JUMPIN' JACK FLASH

WORDS & MUSIC BY MICK JAGGER & KEITH RICHARD

I was born   in a   cross fire hur - ri - cane,
I was raised   by a   tooth-less bear - ded hag.
I was drowned.   I was   washed up and left for   dead.

And I howled   at my ma in the dri - ving   rain.
I was schooled   with a   strap right across   my back.
I fell down   to my   feet and I saw they bled,

To Coda ⊕

But it's al —————— right ————— now. In fact it's a gas —

But it's al————————right.———— I'm Jumpin' Jack Flash. It's a

gas, gas, gas.

1

Fine

2

D.C. al Coda

⊕ CODA

C7 (sus4)   C   C7 (sus4)   C

And I   frowned   at the   crumbs of a crust of   bread.

C7 (sus4)   C   C7 (sus4)   C

I was crowned   with a   spike right through my   head.

D.%. al Fine

LADY JANE

WORDS & MUSIC BY MICK JAGGER & KEITH RICHARD

LET'S SPEND THE NIGHT TOGETHER

WORDS & MUSIC BY MICK JAGGER & KEITH RICHARD

Don't you wor-ry 'bout what's on your mind__ (Oh my. Da da da da__
I feel so strong that I can't dis-guise__ (Oh my. Let's spend the night
This does-n't hap-pen to me ev-'ry day__ (Oh my. Let's spend the night

__ da da__ da) I'm in no hur-ry I can take my time__ (Oh
__ to-geth-er) But I just can't a-pol-o-gise__ (Oh
__ to-geth-er) No ex-cu-ses of-fered an-y way__ (Oh

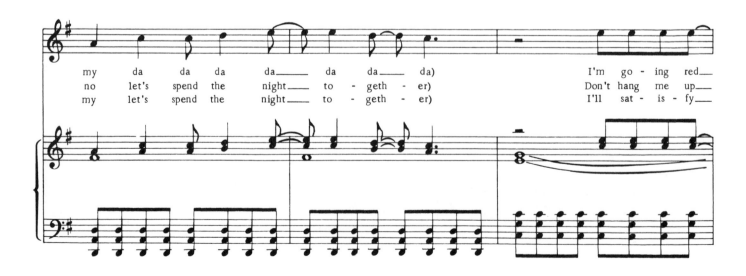

my da da da da__ da da__ da) I'm go-ing red__
no let's spend the night__ to-geth-er) Don't hang me up__
my let's spend the night__ to-geth-er) I'll sat-is-fy

D.C. and repeat from ⊕ to ⊕ ad lib. and fade

MIDNIGHT RAMBLER

WORDS & MUSIC BY MICK JAGGER & KEITH RICHARD

Did you
hear a-bout the mid-night _____ ram - bler? _____ (-) ev-'ry-bo-dy got to go
talk-ing 'bout the mid-night _____ gam - bler, _____ the one you ne-ver seen be-fore

hear a-bout____ the mid-night__ram - bler?____   well   ho - ney, it's no rock and roll

show. Well I'm a - talk-ing 'bout the mid-night ——— ram - bler, ——— yeah, — the

one you ne-ver seen be-fore. ———

say I ____ told you ____ so____ Well won't you
fist right thru'your steel plate door.__

Did you hear a-bout the mid-night ram-bler?__ He'll leave his

foot-prints up and down your_ hall.____ A-did you hear a-bout_ the mid-night_ gam-

PAINT IT BLACK

WORDS AND MUSIC BY MICK JAGGER, KEITH RICHARD,
BILL WYMAN, CHARLIE WATTS AND BRIAN JONES.

RUBY TUESDAY

WORDS & MUSIC BY MICK JAGGER & KEITH RICHARD

She would nev-er say where she came from___
ques - tion why she needs to be so free___
There's no time to lose I heard her say___ She 'll

Am C F G C

Yes - ter-day___ don't mat-ter if it's gone___
Tell you it's___ the on - ly way to be___
cash your dreams___ be - fore they slip a - way___

Am C F C G

While the sun is bright___ or in the dark - est night___ No one knows,
She just can't be chained___ to a life where noth - ing's gained___ And noth-ing's lost___
Dy - ing all the time___ lose your dreams and you___ will lose your mind___

Am D7 G Am D7 G

she comes and goes.
at such a cost.
Ain't life un - kind.

C

G

✶ CHORUS

Good - bye Ru - by Tues - day Who could hang a name on you

C G C G C

To Coda ⊕

Last time
D. S. al Coda

When you change with ev - 'ry new day Still I'm gon - na miss you. 2. Don't

C G B♭ F G C G

⊕ *CODA*

G A mi C F C

SATISFACTION

WORDS & MUSIC BY MICK JAGGER & KEITH RICHARD

With a beat

CHORUS

I___ can't get no___ sat - is - fac - tion.___ I___ can't

get no___ sat - is - fac - tion, 'Cause I try, and I

last time (girl___ with ac - tion,)

try, and I try, and I try.___ I can't get no, I can't

get no,

1. When I'm drivin' in my car,___ And that
2. When I'm watch-in' my T. V.,___ And that
3. When I'm rid-in' 'round the world,___ And I'm

man comes on the ra - di - o; And he's tell-in' me more and more___ a-bout some
man comes on to tell - me; How___ white my shirts can be,___ Well, he
do-in' this and I'm sign - in' that; And I'm try-in' to make some girl.___ Who tells me

use - less in - for - ma - tion, Supposed to___ fire my im-ag - i - na - tion. I can't
can't be a man, 'cause he does - n't smoke the___ same cig-a-rettes as me.___ I can't
ba - by, bet-ter come back let - er next week, 'cos you see I'm on a los - ing streak.___ I can't

get no, Oh, no, no, no, Hey, hey, hey.___

SHE'S A RAINBOW
WORDS & MUSIC BY MICK JAGGER & KEITH RICHARD

Comb-ing col-ours in the air ev'-ry - where, She comes in

Eb   Bb

co lours. _____

rit. -----------

F7   Bb

rit. -------------------- a tempo

Have you seen her dressed in blue?
                        gold?

See the sky in front of
Like a queen in days of

rit. -------------------- a tempo

Bb   F7

you,
old,

And her face is like   a sail, a speck of white so fair and
She shoots co-lours all a - round, like a sun - set   go - ing

STREET FIGHTING MAN

WORDS & MUSIC BY MICK JAGGER & KEITH RICHARD

Mod. Rock

Ev - 'ry-where I hear the sound of march-ing, charg-ing feet, Oh, Boy. 'Cause

sum-mer's here and the time is right for fight - ing in the street, Oh, Boy. But

what can a poor boy do ex - cept to sing for a Rock'N'Roll Band 'cause in sleep-y Lon - don

SYMPATHY FOR THE DEVIL

WORDS & MUSIC BY MICK JAGGER & KEITH RICHARD

Please al - low me to in - tro - duce my - self,__ I'm a man of wealth and taste.__ I've been a - round for long, Long years__ stol - en man - y a man's__ soul and faith. I was a - round when Je -

ev - ry cop__ is a crim - i - nal and all the sin-ners, Saints.__

As heads is tails,__ Just call me Lu - ci - fer 'cause I'm in

need of some re - straint.__ So if you meet me, Have some

court - es - y__ have some sym-pa - thy and some taste. Use all__

STAR STAR

WORDS & MUSIC BY MICK JAGGER & KEITH RICHARD

If I ev - er get back to fun ci - ty girl___ I'm

gon - na make you scream all night___ 2. Hon - Yeah you were

star buck - er star buck - er star buck - er star buck - er star___

Yeah star buck - er star buck - er star buck - er star buck - er star

2. Honey, honey call me on the telephone
   I know you are moving out to Hollywood with your can of tasty foam
   All those beat up friends of mine
   Got to get them in my book
   And lead guitars and movie stars, get their toes beneath my hook
   Yeah you were starbucker, starbucker star
   Starbucker, starbucker star
   Starbucker, starbucker star.

3. Yes I heard about your polaroids now that's what I call obscene
   Your tricks with fruit were kinda cute
   Now that really is a scene
   Honey I miss your two tone kisses, legs wrapped around me tight
   If ever I get back to New York
   I'm gonna make you scream all night
   Yeah starbucker, starbucker star
   Starbucker, starbucker star
   Starbucker, starbucker star.

4. At the draw I got mad at you for giving it to Steve McQueen
   And you and me made a pretty pair falling through the silver screen
   Now baby I am open to anything I don't know where to draw the line
   Well I am making bets that you gonna get your man before he dies
   You were starbucker, starbucker, starbucker star
   Were starbucker, starbucker, starbucker star
   Were starbucker, starbucker, starbucker star
   Were starbucker, starbucker, starbucker star

19TH NERVOUS BREAKDOWN

WORDS & MUSIC BY MICK JAGGER & KEITH RICHARD

You're the kind of per-son you meet at cer-tain dis-mal dull af-fairs Cen-tre
were a child you were treat-ed kind but nev-er brought up right You were

of a crowd talk-ing much too loud run-ning up and down the stairs It seems to me that
o-ver spoilt with a thou-sand toys and still you cried all night Your mo-ther who neg-

you have seen too much in too few years And though you try you just can't hide your
-lec-ted you owes a mil-lion dol-lars tax Your fa-ther's still per-fect-ing ways of

TUMBLING DICE

WORDS & MUSIC BY MICK JAGGER & KEITH RICHARD

UNDER MY THUMB
WORDS & MUSIC BY MICK JAGGER & KEITH RICHARD

10/93 (16372)